Let's Get Ready for Reading

A Guide to Help Kids Become Readers

Toronto Public Library

annick press
toronto + berkeley

© 2017 Toronto Public Library (text)

Cover art/design by Pixel Hive Studio
Designed by Pixel Hive Studio

Annick Press Ltd.

We acknowledge the support of the Canada Council for the Arts, the Ontario Arts Council, and the participation of the Government of Canada/la participation du gouvernement du Canada for our publishing activities.

Cataloging in Publication

    Let's get ready for reading : a guide to help kids become readers / Toronto Public Library.

Previously published: Toronto: Toronto Public Library, 2012.
Previous edition had subtitle: A fun and easy guide to help kids become readers.
ISBN 978-1-55451-903-3 (paperback)

    1. Reading (Early childhood). 2. Reading--Parent participation. 3. Children--Books and reading. I. Toronto Public Library, author

LB1050.2 L485 2017   649'.58   C2016-906260-0

Published in the U.S.A. by Annick Press (U.S.) Ltd.
Distributed in Canada by University of Toronto Press.
Distributed in the U.S.A. by Publishers Group West.

Printed in China

Visit us at: www.annickpress.com
Visit Toronto Public Library at: www.torontopubliclibrary.ca

Also available in e-book format.

Please visit www.annickpress.com/ebooks.html
for more details. Or scan

Table of Contents

Welcome to Ready for Reading!

You are your child's first and best teacher, so the time you spend every day talking, reading, singing, playing, and writing with your child lays the foundation for a love of learning that will last a lifetime.

Toronto Public Library is pleased to share this unique resource, based on the latest early literacy research, to help parents, caregivers, and children get started on their reading adventures together. We have gathered together a selection of rhymes, activities, favorite books, and more to show you how fun and easy it can be to help children build the important skills they need to get ready for reading and for success in school.

And remember, at the library, we're always here to help, so just ask. Our experts in early literacy are ready to support you and your family as your child begins their learning journey.

Vickery Bowles.

Vickery Bowles
City Librarian
Toronto Public Library

You are your child's first and best teacher.

This guide has lots of ideas to help you get your child ready for reading.

It's never too early to start and it's never too late to learn more.

Talk
Read
Sing
Play
Write

These everyday activities that you do with your child help to build important pre-reading skills.

Talk

Read together and encourage your child to talk about the story and pictures. Ask questions, like what they think might happen next.

Read

Read everywhere, anytime and anything—books (of course!), signs, labels, even cereal boxes! It's the best way to help your child become a strong reader.

Sing

Have fun and don't worry about how you sound! From birth, your child loves to hear your voice. Singing helps your child hear the sounds in words and builds her vocabulary.

Play

Play games. Play with words and make music and rhymes. Play make-believe and create new worlds and fabulous stories. Play is how children learn, and how they come to understand their world.

Write

Show your child how you write your shopping list, and let him "write" one too. Writing helps him learn that letters and words represents sounds, and that print has meaning.

 Activities in action!
See these tips and more come to life by checking out our videos at **torontopubliclibrary.ca/ readyforreading**.

Liking Books

Children who enjoy books will want to learn to read

- Enjoying books together every day is the first step toward developing a love of reading. Start the day your child is born.

- Positive, fun, and playful experiences with books and stories foster a desire to read and encourage your child to keep trying to read.

- This chapter offers some ideas and activities to help you give your child a love of books.

Developmental milestones

Each child is unique, but you may observe these signs that your child is interested in language, books, and reading.

Babies:

• Respond to your voice and facial expressions

• Start to look at picture books with interest and try pointing to objects

Toddlers:

• May pretend to read books themselves

• Begin to understand how to handle books

Preschoolers:

• Enjoy listening to and talking about storybooks

• Make attempts to read and write

Action rhymes

Children love rhymes with actions.

ZOOM, ZOOM, ZOOM

Here's a rhyme that you can do with any child. Gently bounce or rock your baby and lift her into the air at "Blast off." Older children can learn to follow the actions.

Zoom, zoom, zoom,	*(Standing, rub hands upward)*
We're going to the moon.	*(Point up into the sky)*
Zoom, zoom, zoom,	*(Standing, rub hands upward)*
We're going to the moon.	*(Point up into the sky)*
If you want to take a trip,	
Climb aboard my rocket ship.	*(Pretend to climb a ladder)*
Zoom, zoom, zoom,	*(Standing, rub hands upward)*
We're going to the moon.	
10, 9, 8, 7, 6, 5, 4, 3, 2, 1,	*(Slowly crouch down)*
Blast off!!!	*(Jump up!)*

 ONLINE VIDEO
Visit **torontopubliclibrary.ca/readyforreading** to view video performances of fun rhymes like this one.

 DID YOU KNOW?
A child's interest in reading is an important predictor of later reading achievement.

Have fun reading!

Bring a sense of adventure to your reading. Read with humor, expression, and enthusiasm.

- Give the story characters different voices. Make your voice loud or soft, high or low. Read faster or slower to fit the story, and add pauses for dramatic effect. Play with adding sounds.

- Try using a puppet or stuffed animal to help read or tell a story.

- Involve the whole family in stories.

First & Best

※ This symbol identifies Toronto Public Library's annual top picks of Canadian children's books for building reading readiness. Because the first books you share with your child should also be the best! See pages 66–67. Learn more at **torontopubliclibrary. ca/readyforreading.**

Me and My Brother
❦ Ruth Ohi, 2007

Brothers can be best friends, partners in crime, and sworn enemies, all in the space of an hour. A great exploration of sibling relationships that are so important and enduring.

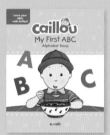

※ Caillou: My First ABC Alphabet Soup
❦ Anne Paradis, 2015

Caillou's dad has served alphabet soup, but it's too hot. While they wait for it to cool, Dad proposes a letter-hunt game.

Red is Best
❦ Kathy Stinson, 1982
Illus. Robin Baird Lewis

No one understands the perfection of red like this little girl.

❦ Canadian   ※ First & Best selection

Start a conversation

One way to engage your child in a book is to start a conversation about what you're reading.

- Relate the pictures and the story to your child's own experiences. For example: "What happened when we went to the park?"

- Talk about what the characters are doing or feeling.

- Share a book together without actually reading it.

DID YOU KNOW?
Playing is how children learn. Share with your child all the wonderful rhymes, books, and songs your parents shared with you as a child in your home language.

Language is fun

Songs and rhymes are playful ways to make language and learning fun.

TOMMY THUMBS

Have your child copy your actions.

Tommy Thumbs are up,	*(Wiggle thumbs up)*
And Tommy Thumbs are down.	*(Wiggle thumbs down)*
Tommy Thumbs are dancing all around the town.	*(Wiggle thumbs)*
Dance them on your shoulders,	*(Tap thumbs on shoulders)*
Dance them on your head.	*(Tap thumbs on head)*
Dance them on your knees,	*(Tap thumbs on knees)*
And tuck them into bed.	*(Hide thumbs in fists)*

OPEN THEM, SHUT THEM

Open them, shut them,

Open them, shut them,

Give a little clap, clap, clap.

Open them, shut them,

Open them, shut them,

Put them in your lap, lap, lap.

Creep them, creep them,

Creep them, creep them,

Right up to your chin, chin, chin.

Open wide your little mouth...

But do not put them in!

Make reading time special

Sharing a book is an opportunity to bond with your child and to show him that reading is important.

- Find a cosy place to read and, if possible, read with your child in your lap, or sit close and cuddle. Being close makes reading together a warm and happy experience that your child looks forward to.

- Tell your child how reading with him is the favorite part of your day.

- Remember to smile at your child while you are reading.

Play peekaboo games

With peekaboo games, you may cover either your face or your child's face. Another way to play peek-a-boo is to hide behind something and pop out while saying, "peekaboo!" Not only do children love playing the peekaboo game, they love peekaboo rhymes, songs, and books as well.

PEEKABOO SONG

Sing to the tune of "Frère Jacques."

Peekaboo! Peekaboo!	*(Cover face with hands)*
I see you! I see you!	*(Open hands to uncover face)*
I see your button nose.	*(Point to your nose or child's nose)*
I see your tiny toes.	*(Point to child's feet)*
I see you. Peekaboo!	*(Cover and uncover face)*

Personalize this rhyme by using your child's name in place of "you."

Where's the Elephant?
Barroux, 2016
A hide-and-seek picture book that tackles urban development and the impact it has on animal habitats.

Old MacDonald Had a Truck
Steve Goetz, 2016
Illus. Eda Kaban

A new twist on a classic song/story featuring pigs in hard hats using excavators and a woman at home handling a steamroller. Rollicking good fun.

Actual Size
Steve Jenkins, 2004
This engaging non-fiction book introduces children to some of the wonders of our natural world.

Make your own books. Make them personal.

- Children love hearing stories about when you were a child. Create a photo album of people that your child knows. Share stories with your child about the people in the pictures.

- To create a book on a subject that interests your child, start by collecting pictures from old magazines, advertisements, or newspapers.

- If possible, let your child choose the pictures and help cut them out. Your child can help sort them and glue them onto sheets of paper.

- Label the pictures and make a cover sheet for the book's title. Staple the pages together and let your child tell you stories about the pictures in his book.

How to choose books your child will love

It's not surprising that children will love to read if they love what they're reading. Here are suggestions for how to choose books your child will love:

- Follow your child's developing interests. Share picture books, information books, and true stories with your child.

- Ask your public librarian to help you find books on the subject your child is interested in. It's a chance for you and your child to learn together.

- Let your child choose her own books and stories to read, to borrow from the library, or to buy.

- Books with cut-outs, lift-the-flaps, pop-ups, or anything that moves are favorites. Kids love them! Look for touch-and-feel features, scratch-and-sniff elements, and sounds.

- For babies, board books are sturdier and more durable. They tend to be small and easy for small hands to handle. Cloth books, as well as those with a mirror, can also be good choices for babies.

Read every day

Share books with your child, even your baby, every day and throughout the day.

- It's helpful to create a special time for reading, such as after dinner, before naps, or at bedtime. Make books and stories a part of your child's daily routine.

- Read together when you are both in a good mood. Reading happily even for a short time will help develop your child's interest in reading.

Ten Little Fingers and Ten Little Toes
Mem Fox, 2008
Illus. Helen Oxenbury
This delightful book celebrates a world of adorable babies.

Tap the Magic Tree
Christie Matheson, 2013
Tap, shake, touch, and wiggle illustrations to transform a lonely apple tree with the seasons.

Over and over again!

Young children love repetition and learn from it. Repeated readings are comforting and build self-confidence. Children are more likely to try to read a book on their own when they are already familiar with the story.

FIVE LITTLE MONKEYS JUMPING ON THE BED

Five little monkeys jumping on the bed,
(Hold up five fingers and move hand up and down)

One fell off and bumped his head!
(Rub head with hand)

Momma called the doctor and the doctor said,
"No more monkeys jumping on the bed."
(Point index finger and move it back and forth)

Repeat rhyme for:

Four little monkeys...

Three little monkeys...

Two little monkeys...

One little monkey...

Momma called the doctor and the doctor said,
"No more monkeys jumping on the bed."
(Point index finger and move it back and forth)

A popular book version of this little finger play by Eileen Christelow is available through your local library branch.

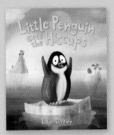

Little Penguin Gets the Hiccups

Tadgh Bentley, 2015

Uh-oh! Little Penguin had some spicy tacos and now has a serious case of the hiccups. He needs your help to get cured. Can you help him?

This Book Just Ate My Dog!

Richard Byrne, 2015

When Bella's dog disappears into the book, Bella calls for help. But when all her helpers disappear too, Bella needs to figure out a way to get her dog back.

Robot Smash!

Stephen Martin, 2015

Illus. Juan Carlos Solon

A powerful robot delights in smashing things until he meets a "super smashy girl robot" laying waste to an entire city.

Singing together

Singing is a fun way to make language come alive for you and your child, and the music makes the words easier to remember. A much-loved song for children of all ages is:

IF YOU'RE HAPPY AND YOU KNOW IT

Have your child copy your actions.

If you're happy and you know it, clap your hands.   *(Clap hands)*

If you're happy and you know it, clap your hands.   *(Clap hands)*

If you're happy and you know it,

And you really want to show it,

If you're happy and you know it, clap your hands.   *(Clap hands)*

Other verses:

… stamp your feet.   *(Stamp feet)*

… shout "hooray!"   *(Raise arms above head)*

When you sing at home, have fun making up your own variations. As your child gets older, let her make up her own new verses too.

"…touch your nose…"

"If you're sad and you know it, cry boo-hoo…"

"If you're dirty and you know it, take a bath…"

"If you're tired and you know it, go to sleep…"

DID YOU KNOW?

Your child learns from you. When your child sees your interest in books and enjoyment in reading, he picks up on your attitude and learns that reading is important—and fun!

Reading in different places adds to the excitement of reading. Here are some fun activities to try:

Fun family fort night

Make a fort at home using pillows and blankets and spend the night reading stories in a fort.

Stories under the stars

Pack a blanket, bug spray, and some snacks and have a reading picnic under the stars at your local park.

If I Had a Triceratops

George O'Connor, 2015

Have you ever wondered what it would take to care for a triceratops? Join a little boy as he imagines having one for a pet.

The Monster at the End of This Book

Jon Stone, 1999

Illus. Michael Smollin

From gluing pages to nailing pages, Grover does everything he can to prevent the reader from turning the page and finding the monster at the end of the book.

The Baby Swap

Jan Ormerod, 2015

Illus. Andrew Joyner

Caroline Crocodile visits the baby shop to try and exchange her baby brother who always drools. Will she find the perfect baby brother, or will she learn to love her own?

Stories everywhere

Place a few tactile books with your baby's toys so that they begin to interact with books. Cloth books and board books with bright colors are great choices.

Clap with your hands over your child's hands to the rhythm of the chants below. You can clap on the syllables or at the end of each line.

HOW MANY DAYS HAS MY BABY TO PLAY?

How many days has my baby to play?

Saturday, Sunday, Monday,

Tuesday, Wednesday, Thursday, Friday,

Saturday, Sunday, Monday.

A B C

Great A, little a,

Bouncing B!

The cat's in the cupboard,

And can't see me.

A Birthday for Cow
Jan Thomas, 2008

Cow's friend wants to surprise him with a birthday cake, but Duck insists on adding a special ingredient. Will Cow be surprised?

Try this at home!

SHARE YOUR FAVORITES

Start a scrapbook to record your child's favorites. Ask your child to draw a picture about their favorite book each week.

- What is your favorite book we read this week?
- What was your favorite part of the story?
- Why did you like this book very much?
- Where is your favorite place to read?
- When is your favorite time to read?

Hearing
Words

Being able to hear the smaller sounds in words helps children sound out written words

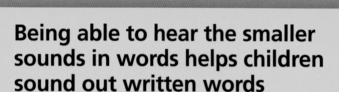

- Recognizing smaller sounds in words and hearing the similarities and differences between sounds that make up words helps develop early literacy skills.

- Talking and singing with your child, sharing finger plays, and reading books with rhymes all help prepare your child to sound out words as she learns to read.

- This chapter offers some ideas and activities to help your child hear the smaller sounds in words.

Developmental milestones

Children learn at different rates. You may observe the following behaviors in your child related to the awareness of sounds in words.

Babies:
- Can copy sounds and actions you make
- Start recognizing words
- Use sounds to get attention

Toddlers:
- Can repeat a familiar rhyme
- Can combine words into simple sentences

Preschoolers:
- Show familiarity with rhyming and beginning sounds
- Participate in rhyming games

Nonsense words

Even silly-sounding nonsense words and rhymes like "hickory dickory," "oopsey-doopsey," and "okey-dokey" are helpful in developing the awareness of sounds in words. Play at making up your own silly words and rhymes.

HICKORY DICKORY DOCK

Hickory dickory dock,	*(Bend arm up at elbow)*
The mouse ran up the clock.	*(Run fingers up arm)*
The clock struck one,	*(Clap loudly once)*
The mouse ran down,	*(Run fingers back down arm)*
Hickory dickory dock.	

The clock struck two, the mouse said, "BOO!"

The clock struck three, the mouse said, "WHEE!"

The clock struck four, the mouse said, "NO MORE!"

"Hickory Dickory Dock" is a rhyme that can be easily adapted. For younger children, you might use just the first verse as a simple bounce. Older children can sway back and forth to the words "Hickory dickory dock" and really act it out.

✔ TIP
Be sure to give a baby's head extra support during bounces until she is strong enough to hold her head steady herself.

DID YOU KNOW?
Most children who have difficulty reading have trouble hearing the smaller sounds in words.

Rhymes and nursery rhyme books

Rhyming helps your child understand that words are made of smaller parts.

- Nursery rhymes are usually short and easy to remember. They make ideal portable "playthings" for you and your child.

- Sing, read, or say rhymes at any time—at bath or change time, while eating, or before bed. Anytime, any place!

- Many collections of nursery rhymes, or Mother Goose rhymes, can be found in your library.

- When choosing nursery rhyme books, a one-rhyme book is ideal for babies, while one rhyme per page works well for toddlers. Preschoolers are ready for more rhymes.

- Make up words that rhyme with your child's name.

❊ **Out Came the Sun: A Day in Nursery Rhymes**
❦ Heather Collins, 2007
This adorable collection of nursery rhymes follows an animal family through their fun-filled day.

❊ **Sing a Song of Mother Goose**
❦ Barbara Reid, 2008
As one of Canada's leading author/illustrators, Barbara Reid brings to life favorite traditional rhymes with her amazing artwork.

Brown Bear, Brown Bear, What Do You See?
Bill Martin, 1967
Illus. Eric Carle
Brown Bear meets up with an assortment of humorously colored animal friends.

❦ Canadian   ❊ First & Best selection

Children and poetry

Sharing nursery rhymes and poetry is one of the best ways to introduce your child to rhyming words.

- For very young babies, try rhymes that involve a gentle touch, such as patting their feet.
- Play with your child by making up short rhymes and poems together.

Hearing sounds

Being able to hear and recognize the beginning, middle, and ending sounds that make up words helps children sound out words when they begin to read.

FROM WIBBLETON TO WOBBLETON

Face your child toward you to see each other's expressions and enjoy bonding. Bounce your child on your knee in time to the rhythm. It's fun to bounce "Wibbleton" toward one side, and "Wobbleton" to the other side. "Fifteen miles" is somewhere in the middle.

From Wibbleton to Wobbleton is 15 miles.

From Wobbleton to Wibbleton is 15 miles.

From Wibbleton to Wobbleton,

From Wobbleton to Wibbleton,

From Wibbleton to Wobbleton is 15 miles.

LEG OVER LEG

This rhyme is good to use while changing a baby's diaper. It can also be used as a bouncing rhyme with your toddler, or acted out by your three-to-five-year-old.

With baby on table, hold ankles and cross legs; lift legs on last line.

Leg over leg, the dog went to Dover.

When he came to a fence—

Jump! He went over.

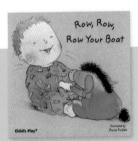

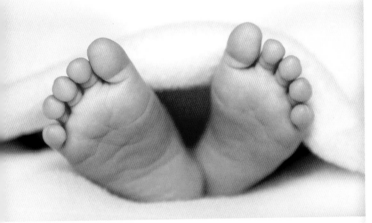

Row, Row, Row Your Boat
Illus. Annie Kubler, 2003

A wonderfully illustrated board book of the familiar rhyme with fun new verses to keep babies laughing.

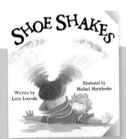

Shoe Shakes
✤ Loris Lesynski, 2007
Illus. Michael Martchenko

A celebration of feet in motion certain to get children tapping their toes and stomping their feet. This collection of 10 poems is a surefire winner.

DID YOU KNOW?
Repetition strengthens connections in your child's developing brain. Repeat rhymes and songs so your child can become familiar with them and really master them.

Listening and rhythm

When you march, dance, or sing together, you break up words into smaller sounds.

- Add actions as you sing a song or recite a poem. Actions help children break down language into separate words.

- Add clapping, tapping, drumming, bouncing, walking, marching, jumping, and dancing activities to language. For example, clap your baby's hands or have your toddler clap along to the rhyme, music, or song.

- Say a word to your child and ask him to count the number of sounds he hears, and show the number by holding up his fingers, jumping up and down, or clapping. For example, "porcupine" has three sounds or syllables—"por-cu-pine." Your child would jump three times.

Rhythm instruments

If you don't have a rattle to shake to the rhythm of the music or song, you can make one. Seal beans, uncooked rice, cereal, or popcorn in a small unbreakable container to use as a shaker or maraca. Play with your child and say "shake, shake" each time your child shakes the container.

Rhyme & rhythm

This rhyme is great to clap along to. See if your child will copy your actions. With older children, try clapping your hands against their hands. In place of clapping, you can tap your knees or stamp your feet to the rhythm. Rub your tummy, smile, and say "yummy, yummy" at the end.

PEASE PORRIDGE HOT

Pease porridge hot.
Pease porridge cold.
Pease porridge in the pot,
Nine days old.
Some like it hot.
Some like it cold.
Some like it in the pot,
Nine days old.

DID YOU KNOW?
Playing fun listening games like "Simon Says" is good for improving your child's listening skills.

Farmyard Beat
Lindsey Craig, 2011
Illus. Marc Brown
What's better than a dance-a-thon—a farmyard dance-a-thon, of course! But what happens when all the noise wakes up Farmer Sue?

Pete the Cat and His Four Groovy Buttons
Eric Litwin, 2012
Illus. James Dean
Pete the Cat loves the buttons on his shirt so much that he makes up a song about them. Even as the buttons pop off, he still finds a reason to sing.

❋ Ladybugs Have Lots of Spots
Sheryl and Simon Shapiro, 2013
Using poetry and photographs, children are encouraged to explore what is round, from the spots on a ladybug to the wheels on a car.

Whispering games

Practice listening skills. Whisper from different parts of the room and ask your child where the sound is coming from.

DID YOU KNOW?

While you read together, your child may not seem to be paying attention, but she may surprise you with what she has learned.

Sing!

Singing songs is an excellent way to help children hear the smaller, different sounds in words because each syllable in a word often gets its own musical note.

- Don't worry about how you sound—from birth, your child loves to hear your voice.

- Sing songs or rhymes in the language that is most comfortable for you. Young children don't need to understand the words for these moments together to be learning experiences.

- Songs and music also help your child learn rhythm.

Throughout the day

Add songs, rhyming, and language games to your activities throughout the day.

- Books that celebrate sounds and noises that are all around give young children practice listening.

- Books of simple, familiar songs are good choices for young listeners.

DID YOU KNOW?
Playing with words like cat/hat/bat in songs and rhymes builds the ability to hear the smaller sounds in words.

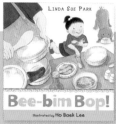

Bee-bim Bop!
Linda Sue Park, 2005
Illus. Ho Baek Lee
A little girl helps her mother shop for and prepare a favorite meal of delicious Bee-bim Bop.

Llama Llama Red Pajama
Anna Dewdney, 2005
After being tucked into bed by his mother, baby llama doesn't want to be left alone. This reassuring tale is told in rhyme.

Eat your words

Using crackers, cereal, or another food, say a word and ask your child to eat the same number of items as the sounds in the word. For example, "bookmark" has two sounds, so your child would eat two crackers.

Try tongue twisters

Tongue twisters are useful for encouraging children to hear the similar sound at the beginning of many words. Books with alliteration are also fun.

PETER PIPER

Peter Piper picked a peck of pickled peppers.

A peck of pickled peppers Peter Piper picked.

If Peter Piper picked a peck of pickled peppers,

Where's the peck of pickled peppers Peter Piper picked?

Song writing

Make up your own words and verses to familiar songs throughout the day and have fun acting them out.

RING AROUND THE ROSIE

Ring around the rosie, a pocketful of posies,
(Children hold hands and go around in a circle)

A-husha! A-husha! We all fall down!
(Everybody sits on the floor)

Picking up the daisies, picking up the daisies,
(Children pretend to pick flowers)

A-husha! A-husha! We all stand up!
(Everybody jumps up)

Search and find

Search and find games help connect objects with the words. Find a few of your child's favorite things, put them on a tray, and ask your child to listen and pick up different things as you say them. You can ask them to pick up the brown teddy bear, something that makes the "ssss" sound, or something that is purple.

We're going on a sound hunt

Visit a park, library, backyard, or anywhere you hear different sounds in your house. Put your baby on your lap facing you and listen quietly. When you hear a sound, make an excited face and ask your child, "Did you hear that? It is a _____."

With older children, ask them to close their eyes and listen carefully. Then ask them, "What did you hear?" "What else do you hear?"

Animal sound match

Play at matching an animal with the sound it makes. When children can imitate animal noises they are also learning to hear the sounds in words, developing the skill that helps them sound out words when learning to read.

OLD MACDONALD HAD A FARM

Old MacDonald had a farm, E-I-E-I-O.

And on his farm he had a cow, E-I-E-I-O.

With a moo, moo here and a moo, moo there,

Here a moo, there a moo,

Everywhere a moo, moo.

Old MacDonald had a farm, E-I-E-I-O.

You can continue adding as many animals as you like, replacing the cow, but following the pattern.

For example:

…And on his farm he had a pig, E-I-E-I-O.

With an oink, oink here and an oink, oink there…

We're Going on a Bear Hunt
Michael Rosen, 1989
Illus. Helen Oxenbury

Brave hunters must overcome many obstacles before they find the fierce bear in its cave.

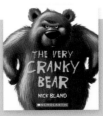

The Very Cranky Bear
Nick Bland, 2009
A rhyming story, with hilarious illustrations, about four friends who try to cheer up a cranky bear.

Sheep in a Jeep
Nancy Shaw, 2003
Illus. Margot Apple
Beep! Beep! There's a jeep full of sheep coming.

Listen up!

One of the most important skills your child can learn is how to listen. Try some of these activities to help her practice listening:

Play Teddy Bear says

This is a fun game that helps teach your child to listen closely. Call out simple instructions for your child to do, such as:

Teddy Bear says, touch your toes.

Teddy Bear says, touch your nose.

Teddy Bear says, sit down.

Then, say some of the instructions without saying "Teddy Bear says," such as:

Turn around.

Touch your ears.

Touch your shoulders.

Ask your child to only follow the instructions if they hear "Teddy Bear says" before the instructions. If your child does an action when you don't say, "Teddy Bear says," then it's their turn to become the teddy bear and call out the actions for you.

Play with nursery rhymes

- Read or sing a nursery rhyme and ask your child to listen for the rhyme. For example, try reciting "Hickory, dickory, dock. The mouse ran up the clock!" and point out the rhyming words "dock" and "clock." Then try a different rhyme and ask your child to find the rhyming words.

- As a variation, say most of the rhyme, but leave out the rhyming last word and ask your child to provide it. For example, "Jack and Jill went up the _____" (hill). Or try, "Up above the world so high, like a diamond in the _____" (sky).

♣ Sing a Song of Bedtime

Barbara Reid, 2015

A collection of beautifully illustrated classic rhymes and lullabies to help your child sleep.

The Silver Moon: Lullabies and Cradle Songs

Jack Prelutsky, 2013

Illus. Jui Ishida

Sweet, soothing, and original bedtime lullabies and cradle songs that will make your baby fall asleep, and maybe you too!

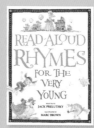

Read-Aloud Rhymes for the Very Young

Jack Prelutsky, 1986

Illus. Marc Brown

Over 200 beautifully illustrated poems and rhymes for a wide range of childhood moments.

Here are some more chants that can help children hear words that rhyme which will build their rhyming vocabulary.

RAIN, RAIN, GO AWAY

Rain, rain, go away,

Come again another day.

JACK BE NIMBLE

Jack be nimble, Jack be quick,

Jack jump over the candlestick.

THERE WAS A LITTLE MAN

(Hold the baby's hands in yours and clap the rhythm of this chant)

There was a little man, whose color was of tan.

I found him in the kitchen in an old tin pan.

Although I did not hate him, I broke him up and ate him.

It did not hurt him one little bit.

Because that little man, whose color was of tan,

Was a gingerbread man!

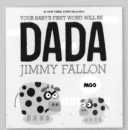

Your Baby's First Word Will Be DADA

Jimmy Fallon, 2015

Illus. Miguel Ordóñez

Dads all secretly want their children to say "Dada" before "Mama." Can these animal dads succeed in the race of "mama" versus "dada"?

Try this at home!

LET'S SING AND DANCE

Singing and dancing are great ways to help words come alive for children. Talk to your child about their favorite songs, rhymes, activities, and books and write them on a bookmark. Bring this bookmark out before you read together and sing or act out one of the songs or rhymes.

- What is your favorite happy song?
- What is your favorite silly song?
- What is your favorite animal song?
- What is your favorite rhyme?
- What is your favorite book?
- What is your favorite game to play?

Knowing Words

Knowing many words helps children recognize written words and understand what they read

- Vocabulary is about knowing the names of things, feelings, ideas, and concepts (like "more or less", and "before or after").

- Hearing and understanding many words helps children sound them out when they are learning to read.

- This chapter offers some ideas and activities to help your child learn more words.

Developmental milestones

Vocabulary begins to develop at birth and continues to grow throughout life. Here are some common stages in building vocabulary.

Babies:
- Can understand the names of some familiar people and objects
- Babble and try to "talk" with you

Toddlers:
- Can use words to express desires and feelings
- Are familiar with the main parts of the body

Preschoolers:
- Know the names of familiar animals
- Can name common objects in picture books
- Can create longer sentences

New words

Rhymes and books help teach many new words that children may not hear in everyday conversation.

TEN LITTLE FINGERS

I have 10 little fingers,	*(Hold up all 10 fingers)*
And they all belong to me.	*(Point to self)*
I can make them do things,	
Would you like to see?	
I can shut them up tight;	*(Make fists)*
I can open them wide;	*(Extend fingers)*
I can put them together;	*(Clasp hands)*
And I can make them all hide.	*(Hide hands behind back)*
I can put them up high;	*(Reach hands above head)*
I can put them down low;	*(Touch floor with hands)*
I can fold them together,	*(Clasp hands and intertwine fingers)*
And hold them just so.	*(Place hands in lap)*

WHAT ARE THESE FOR?

Hold up both hands asking, "What are these for? Hands are for folding." Fold your hands together. "And hands are for clapping!" Clap hands together.

Encourage your child to copy your words and actions.

Continue with other body parts:

Toes—tapping, tickling, etc.

Eyes—sleeping, looking, etc.

Nose—sniffing, sneezing, etc.

DID YOU KNOW?
Children develop larger vocabularies the more time they spend talking and reading with family members.

Babies talk

Start talking to your baby in your home language on the day he is born.

- By babbling, babies learn to make sounds with their own voices. Encourage your baby to become more vocal by responding to his coos, gurgles, and grunts to promote language development.

- When your child says "Aaah," say it back to her, and turn the sounds into real words. Encourage your child to copy you too. You'll help your child recognize which sounds form language, and develop her vocabulary before she can talk.

- When your child babbles or talks, listen carefully and answer. Even if you don't know what he means or he doesn't have the words to answer, talk to your child and ask him lots of questions.

Nursery rhymes

Rhymes are an excellent way to build vocabulary.

I'M A LITTLE TEAPOT

I'm a little teapot, short and stout.

Here is my handle, and here is my spout.

(Right hand is on hip, left arm is bent at the elbow with hand pointing to the side)

When I get all steamed up, hear me shout.

Just tip me over and pour me out.

Wiggle Your Toes
Karen Katz, 2006
A great board book that helps children identify different parts of the body, from wiggling their toes to pointing to their noses.

Eyes, Nose, Fingers, and Toes: A First Book All About You
Judy Hindley, 1999
Illus. Brita Granström
It's fun to learn the names of all the parts of your body.

Where is the Green Sheep?
Mem Fox, 2004
Illus. Judy Horacek
Our green sheep must be here somewhere... Let's look!

Little Bird's Bad Word
Jacob Grant, 2015
A wonderful story that teaches children about how some words can hurt the feelings of others.

Play with music

Sing throughout the day and make up your own silly songs to introduce new words.

- New words can be easier to learn when they rhyme or are put to music.

- Many activities can be sung to the tune of "Here We Go 'Round the Mulberry Bush." For example, in the bathtub, wash your child while singing "This is the way I wash my face…," adding your own verses.

- Let your child help make up new words to familiar songs.

DID YOU KNOW?
Books offer richer vocabulary than ordinary daily conversation. Your child hears more new words when you read books with her every day.

Parts of the body

Some of the first words babies learn are for different parts of their bodies. Rhymes and songs are a fun way to learn, in any language.

HEAD AND SHOULDERS

Sing to the tune of "London Bridge Is Falling Down." Have your child copy you and touch each body part.

Head and shoulders,

Knees and toes, knees and toes, knees and toes.

Head and shoulders, knees and toes,

Eyes, ears, mouth, and nose.

You can sing this with your baby, gently touching the parts of the body. Toddlers and preschoolers enjoy this rhyme as an action song. This rhyme is fun to perform faster and faster and faster.

. . . .

HANA, HANA, HANA A Japanese face poem
Touch the body part as you say the word for it.

Hana, hana, hana.	*(Touch nose)*
Kutchi, kutchi, kutchi.	*(Touch mouth)*
Mimi, mimi, mimi.	*(Touch ears)*
Mei.	*(Point to eyes)*

ONLINE VIDEO
Visit **torontopubliclibrary.ca/readyforreading** to view video performances of fun rhymes like this one.

Use new words

Practice saying new words together.

- Take the time to stop and explain unfamiliar words when reading or speaking with your child.

- Speak clearly when introducing new words.

- When a word has more than one meaning, talk about the different meanings.

- When talking with your child, use a variety of descriptive words.

- Use specific words instead of words like "it," "here," or "there."

- For familiar words in a book, rhyme, or song, think of a new word that has a similar meaning.

- When a child is learning a new word, use it often throughout the day. Be patient as you re-read the same story over and over.

DID YOU KNOW?
Repeating new words is important. Repetition helps your child's brain link sound and meaning.

The Very Hungry Caterpillar
Eric Carle, 1969
A very hungry caterpillar eats its way through the pages of this wholly irresistible book.

The Book With No Pictures
B.J. Novak, 2014
This book invites the adult reader to read aloud increasingly silly text, to the absolute enjoyment of the child listening—statements such as "My head is made of blueberry pizza."

☀ One Watermelon Seed
🍁 Celia Barker Lottridge, 2008
Illus. Karen Patkau
Count the seeds to plant and their bountiful crops in Max and Josephine's garden.

One Word from Sophia
Jim Averbeck, 2015
Illus. Yasmeen Ismail
A charming book both children and adults will enjoy about little Sophia, who makes a case for why she should get a giraffe for her birthday.

What's for lunch?

You'll discover all sorts of new words when you cook with your child. What fantastic meals can your child invent for you? New experiences usually introduce new vocabulary.

🍁 Canadian   ☀ First & Best selection

While reading

Children learn best by doing—and they love doing things with YOU.

- While sharing books with your child, encourage her to talk about the story and pictures, instead of just listening to you read.

- Invite him to participate by asking questions. Ask, "What's that?" and point to and name pictures in a book.

- Ask questions like, "Where is the dog?" or, "What is the doggy doing?" Then add more describing words to what your child says, including the character's feelings, even if those words are not used in the book.

- Focus on a few new words in each book you read together. Practice saying them together and repeat them in other situations.

I HAD A LITTLE TURTLE

I had a little turtle,	*(Make a fist with thumb sticking out)*
He lived in a box.	*(Cup hands together for a box)*
He swam in a puddle.	*(Wiggle hand for swimming)*
He climbed on the rocks.	*(Fingers climb up other fist)*
He snapped at a mosquito,	*(Snap fingers)*
He snapped at a flea,	*(Snap)*
He snapped at a minnow,	*(Snap)*
And he snapped at me!	*(Snap)*
He caught the mosquito,	*(Clap, gulp)*
He caught the flea,	*(Clap, gulp)*
He caught the minnow,	*(Clap, gulp)*
But he didn't catch me!	*(Wag pointer finger back and forth)*

ROW, ROW, ROW YOUR BOAT

Support your baby against your chest and rock back and forth in rhythm; sit older child facing you, hold her hands, and rock back and forth.

Row, row, row your boat,

Gently down the stream.

Merrily, merrily, merrily, merrily,

Life is but a dream.

Row, row, row your boat down the jungle stream,

If you see a crocodile, don't forget to scream!

 ONLINE VIDEO

Visit **torontopubliclibrary.ca/readyforreading** to view video performances of fun rhymes like this one.

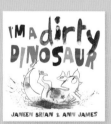

I'm a Dirty Dinosaur
Janeen Brian, 2013
Illus. Ann James
A brightly colored story about a dinosaur who likes mud and being dirty, with fun actions for kids.

Big, Bigger, Biggest!
Nancy Coffelt, 2009
After reading this colorful book, your vocabulary will be jumbo, gigantic, colossal!

Talking is important

The more you talk with your child, the more words they will learn.

- Talk about and explain what you're doing and what's going on around you.

- Point at and name items as you see them.

- Whether you're bathing your child or taking a walk, use words that describe the actions and the things around you. Talk about all the senses involved.

- Help your child learn new words for concepts and ideas, as well as objects. More/less and before/after are examples of concepts.

- Talk about feelings—yours and your child's. Having the words to express feelings may help reduce your child's frustration.

DID YOU KNOW?
Most two-year-olds can understand 300 to 500 words, and most children enter school knowing between 3,000 to 5,000 words.

Play games

You are your child's first and favorite playmate.

MY TURN, YOUR TURN

Face your child. Touch your tummy and say, "Look! Here is Daddy's tummy!" Ask your child, "Do you have a tummy? Where is your tummy?"

Help your child find her tummy. Now, point to her tummy and ask (as if you've forgotten), "What's this again?" This gives your child a chance to name the body part herself. Continue in this way with other body parts.

BRAINSTORMING GAMES

Think of a category such as animals, foods, round things, red things, or things that grow. Take turns with your child thinking of different words that fit into that category.

I SPY GAME

Say, "I spy with my little eye, something that is ...," and ask your child to find something according to a category, like shape, color, or size.

Naming, labeling, and sorting

As your child starts talking, help him find the words for things around him. Make a game of labeling items in your home together. When you are running errands, point out things in the neighborhood and in the shops.

COLLAGE COLLECTION

Make a collection of magazine pictures that are alike in some way. If your child loves pets, collect pictures of dogs, cats, fish, and birds. Label each picture clearly.

SORT YOUR SETS

Find four magazine pictures in the same category and paste each picture on a card. Make five sets of category cards and then mix them up. Ask your child to sort them.

MATCH ME UP

Collect pictures of things your child can easily find in your house: fruits, toys, furniture, or household objects. Show your child a picture. Say, "Oh look! Here is a picture of an apple. I know there is a real apple around here somewhere. Can you find it?" Have your child bring you the object and compare it to the picture.

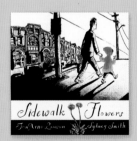

❀ Sidewalk Flowers
JonArno Lawson, 2015
Illus. Sydney Smith
A beautifully illustrated wordless picture book about a girl who collects flowers while walking with her distracted father.

Here Are My Hands
Bill Martin Jr. and John Archambault, 1985
Illus. Ted Rand
A book that helps teach young children the uses of their hands, eyes, ears, nose, and toes.

Beautiful Hands
Kathryn Otoshi, 2015
Illus. Bret Baumgarten
A book that shows that children can make a difference in their worlds, with the help of their little hands.

A picture equals a thousand words

Wordless picture books allow your child to tell a story in their own words using the pictures. Talk to your child about what is happening in the pictures to help him develop his story. Point to pictures in the story and ask your child, "What is this?"

Word plus

Babies often repeat a few words over and over, such as ball. Expand their vocabulary by adding words to common words she can say, such as "Is this your blue ball?"

How do we move?

Children learn through play. The following activity helps children learn new action words while having fun moving.

Ask your toddler, "How do we move?" He might answer walk, run, jump, or any other way. Act out what he says. Play with different actions. Here are some to try:

Let's walk fast.	*(and walk fast)*
Let's walk slow.	*(and walk slow)*
Let's walk like an elephant.	*(put your arms together and sway them in front of your head like an elephant's trunk)*

You can keep playing this game with different actions as long as you have your child's attention.

The story train

This is a fun game that can be played on the way to the grocery store or as an afternoon activity with children four and above.

Start off with one line of a story; for instance, There once lived a dragon in a far away cave. Ask your child to make up the next sentence of the story; for instance, they might say, "One day the dragon woke up and found out he has invisible powers." Keep playing until you finish the story. You can make the story as funny or adventurous as you like.

Hooray for Fish!
Lucy Cousins, 2005
Take a trip with Little Fish as he meets his many different friends.

❧ **Big or Little?**
Kathy Stinson, 2009 *Illus. Toni Goffe*
This book examines the benefits of being big and the frustrations of being small, including the in-between stage when you can read a little but still get lost in the grocery store.

Rhyming Dust Bunnies
Jan Thomas, 2009
As three dust bunnies, Ed, Ned, and Ted, are rhyming away, a fourth bunny, Bob, tries to warn them of danger coming their way.

FIVE LITTLE SPECKLED FROGS

FIVE little speckled frogs,
(Hold up five fingers)

Sat on a speckled log,
(Hold up arms together to make a log)

Eating some most delicious bugs.
(Pretend to eat bugs)

Yum Yum.
(Rub tummy)

One jumped into the pool,
(Hold up one finger and then put hands together and dive forward)

Where it was nice and cool,
(Cross your arms and pretend to shiver)

Then there were FOUR speckled frogs.
(Hold up four fingers)

Glug Glug.

Repeat rhyme for:

FOUR little speckled frogs...

THREE little speckled frogs...

TWO little speckled frogs...

ONE little speckled frog...

Nursery rhymes and songs are wonderful ways to introduce children to new words. Rhymes with silly words can help make words and sentences exciting for children.

THERE'S A WORM AT THE BOTTOM OF MY GARDEN

There's a worm at the bottom of my garden,

And his name is Wiggly Woo.

There's a worm at the bottom of my garden,

And all that he can do,

Is wiggle all day and wiggle all night—

The neighbors say what a terrible fright!

There's a worm at the bottom of my garden,

And his name is Wiggly,

Wig-Wig-Wiggly,

Wig-Wig-Wiggly Woo!

The White Book
Silvia Borando, Elisabetta Pica and Lorenzo Clerici, 2015
Six beautiful birds emerge when a little boy paints the wall pink, but what happens when he paints the wall green?

Try this at home!

WHAT ARE YOUR FAVORITE THINGS?

Let's use lots of words to describe your favorite things.

- What is your favorite animal? What color is it? What sound does it make?

- Who is your favorite person? What are three things that make them so special?

- Where is your favorite place to visit? What makes this place fun?

Telling a Story

Learning to tell a story helps children develop skills in thinking and understanding

- Narrative skills include the ability to describe things; to tell events in order; to tell and retell stories.

- Understanding how stories work, that stories have a beginning, a middle, and an end, is key to reading comprehension.

- This chapter offers some ideas and activities to help your child develop narrative skills and reading comprehension.

Developmental milestones

What comes next? Daily routines, including sharing books, help children learn about the narrative structure of beginning, middle, and end.

Babies:

- May recognize and start to laugh at the first few words of a familiar rhyme
- Anticipate elements of a repeated nursery rhyme
- Enjoy playing peekaboo games

Toddlers:

- May enjoy looking at one book over and over
- Recall events of the day
- May read to stuffed animals or toys

Preschoolers:

- May like to play dress-up
- Can follow directions with three or more steps
- May make predictions based on the pictures in a storybook

DID YOU KNOW?
Children with good narrative skills are better able to understand what they read.

What are narratives?

Narratives are stories with a beginning, a middle, and an end, like these familiar nursery rhymes.

HUMPTY DUMPTY

"Humpty Dumpty" can be chanted, clapped, or bounced, swooping child downward for the "great fall."

Humpty Dumpty sat on a wall.

Humpty Dumpty had a great fall.

All the king's horses,

And all the king's men,

Couldn't put Humpty together again.

Do not weep and worry, do not cry for him I beg,

For though he is not mended, he's a happy scrambled egg.

. . . .

LITTLE BO PEEP

Little Bo Peep,

Has lost her sheep,

And doesn't know where to find them.

Leave them alone,

And they will come home,

Wagging their tails behind them.

ONLINE VIDEO
Visit **torontopubliclibrary.ca/readyforreading** to view a video performance of fun rhymes like this one.

As you read together

Take some time to talk together about the book. It's easy to do.

- You don't have to read a book from cover to cover without stopping. Point to the pictures and ask questions like, "What's this?" or, "What is he doing?" Give your child time to answer, and then praise her efforts. Encourage your child to ask questions, too.

- Add to what your child says. If your child says, "Big truck," you might say, "That's right! The firefighter is driving a big red fire truck!"

- Help your child understand the story. Ask questions such as, "Why do you think the little girl was happy?" or, "What do you think is happening in this picture?" Try to ask questions that can't be answered with "yes" or "no."

- As you talk together, your child practices his language skills. Sharing a book in this way helps build your child's storytelling ability.

Play

Children learn about their world through play. Play gives them the opportunity to learn and practice new skills.

PLAY MAKE-BELIEVE

Encourage play by supplying dress-up clothes and props such as hats, scarves, backpacks, bowls, and containers. As children act out their stories, they are developing narrative skills.

. . . .

SILLY SOUP

Make pretend soup. You will need a saucepan with a lid, a spoon, and some small objects. Say, "Let's make soup!" and ask, "What do you think we should have in our soup?" Let your child choose an object, tell you what it is, and place it in the saucepan. Then it's your turn. Say, "I think we should put some socks in the soup!" When there are three ingredients in the soup, ask your child to stir it and put on the lid. Scratch your head and ask, "Now, what is in our soup? Can you remember what delicious things are in it?" See if your child can recall the ingredients.

. . . .

TELEPHONE TALK

Give your child a toy telephone, or a real phone that isn't in service. Make the phone "ring" and say "Oh! Your telephone is ringing! It must be your friend _____." Then talk to your child on your own telephone. Pretend to be the friend calling, ask your child about her day, and then finish by suggesting that you talk again tomorrow. The next day, play the game again.

What's next?

Look at a book's front cover and ask your child what he thinks the story will be about.

- Look at the pictures, and ask your child what he thinks will happen next. It's fun to read and compare the prediction with what really happens.

- Wordless picture books are great for practicing narrative skills. By giving children a chance to tell a story in their own words, they build their storytelling skills and are encouraged to use descriptive language.

✔ **TIP:** Search for "stories without words" on the library website.

Draw

Have your child draw a picture and tell you about it. Or, after reading a book, your child could draw a picture about something that happened in the story and tell you about that.

❋ *Grumpy Bird*
🍁 Jeremy Tankard, 2007
Even though Bird wakes up so grumpy he doesn't want to fly, his friends stick with him until he feels better.

That Is Not a Good Idea!
Mo Willems, 2013
A dastardly fox and an unsuspecting duck go to the fox's kitchen where only one ingredient for his soup is missing, while a chorus of chicks warn, "That is not a good idea!"

KIND HEARTS
(Sway and move with your child to the rhythm of this poem)

Kind hearts are the gardens,

Kind thoughts are the roots,

Kind words are the flowers,

Kind deeds are the fruits.

Take care of your garden

And keep out the weeds,

Fill it with sunshine

Kind words and kind deeds.

(Henry Wadsworth Longfellow)

JACK AND JILL

Jack and Jill went up the hill

To fetch a pail of water.
(Crawl fingers upward on the baby's arm)

Jack fell down *(Swoop one finger down)*

And broke his crown

And Jill came tumbling after.
(Swoop other finger down)

Choosing books

Books especially good for developing narrative skills have stories that are fun to tell over and over again.

- Let your child fill in a repeated part of a story, or complete a pattern. Encourage participation by saying a repeated line together.

- Ask questions like, "What happened first? And then? What happened in the end?"

- Read and re-read your child's favorite books. Your child becomes more familiar with the story, building her understanding and making it easier for her to retell the story.

DID YOU KNOW?
Telling a story and solving math problems use similar skills.

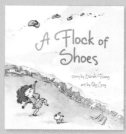

❧ *A Flock of Shoes*
Sarah Tsiang, 2010
Illus. Qin Leng
When Abby refuses to give up her sandals at the end of summer, they take off on their own, sending her postcards from sunny beaches in warmer climes.

The Paper Bag Princess
❧ Robert Munsch, 1980
Illus. Michael Martchenko
When a dragon burns her clothes and captures her fiancé, Princess Elizabeth is forced to wear a paper bag and engage the dragon in a battle of wits.

How to Read a Story
Kate Messner, 2015
Illus. Mark Siegel
If you're not sure how to read a story, then this book is for you! Ten easy steps from finding a book to choosing a comfortable spot to read are outlined.

Shark vs. Train
Chris Barton, 2010
Illus. Tom Lichtenheld
An epic battle between a shark and a train that teaches young readers about competition and fair play.

THIS LITTLE PIGGY
Play on fingers or toes.

This little piggy went to market.

This little piggy stayed home.

This little piggy had roast beef.

This little piggy had none.

And this little piggy ran wee, wee, wee, all the way home.

A tickle is a tiny story building to a predictable climax. A rhyme like "This Little Piggy" allows the anticipation to build for the tickle at the end.

What happens first, next, and last?

Encourage your child to tell you about his day or something that happened, like a birthday party or a special trip.

- Ask questions like, "What happened first? What happened next? What did it look like? What did you like best?"

- Ask your child to tell you about things he does that have a regular order to them, like taking a bath.

- Reading at bedtime is ideal for spending quiet moments with your child. Sharing stories of what happened during the day is a great way to develop narrative skills. It is another opportunity to talk about a child's daily routines, which are stories themselves.

Materials in your own language

Many libraries have collections in different languages. Check with your local library to see if they have a collection in your first language so that you can share stories, music, and movies with your children. Reading and listening in any language helps to develop reading and listening skills in English.

Puppet play

Ask your child to tell you a story using puppets. You can buy hand or finger puppets, or make them. For example, cut out pictures and glue them to Popsicle sticks. Help your child retell or act out her favorite story. Using puppets, toys, dolls, or other props to tell a story may help your child remember it.

HERE IS A BUNNY

This rhyme can be done as a finger play or you could use a rabbit puppet or doll if you have one.

Here is a bunny,	*(Hold up two bent fingers)*
With ears so funny.	*(Wiggle the fingers)*
Here is his hole in the ground.	*(Make circle with thumb and four fingers of other hand)*
When a noise he hears, he pricks up his ears,	*(Straighten two fingers in 'V' shape)*
And jumps in his hole in the ground.	*(Jump fingers into hole on other hand)*

Bedtime game

At any time during the day, play the bedtime game. Together, put a favorite toy to bed. Make the bedtime routine as elaborate as you like. Play versions of this game where your child puts you or another family member to bed.

Describe with your senses

As you go about your day, use all your senses when you talk about what you are doing. For example, as you make dinner, you might say, "Look at all those yellow noodles I'm cooking! Can you hear the water bubbling in the pot? Take a deep breath and smell the red tomato sauce. Mmm… the sauce tastes very spicy!"

Talk. Talk. Talk.

And talk some more.

- Your baby loves to hear your voice. Copy your baby's sounds and listen to the sounds she makes back. Take the time throughout the day to talk with your child about all kinds of things. For example, talk to her about the weather. Ask older children to describe what it's like outside. Complete this sentence: Today the weather is _____.

- Describe daily activities. Talk about what has happened, what is happening, and what will happen during the day. Even with your baby, talk about what you are doing: "Now we're going to change your diaper, and then we are going to have a bottle, and after that we are going to have a nap."

- Your child will listen to the way you describe what you're doing and how you structure your stories.

❧ ***Without You***
Geneviève Côté, 2011
A beautiful story about the ups and downs of friendship. This is a book you won't want to do without!

The End (Almost)
Jim Benton, 2014
Donut the bear wants a story about himself. The author is trying to make it short, while Donut wants it to be more detailed, and tries to change the story.

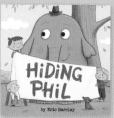

Hiding Phil
Eric Barclay, 2013
How can you hide a large blue elephant so you can take him home? Can parents be convinced that Phil the elephant would make a great addition to the family?

Brief Thief
Michaël Escoffier, 2013
Illus. Kris Di Giacomo
A lizard takes the liberty of using what seems to be some old underpants when he runs out of toilet paper. What happens when an outraged rabbit sees this?

Listen. Listen. Listen.

Make sure your child has lots of opportunities to talk with you.

- Listen attentively as your child tries to tell you something. Even if you cannot understand what your child is saying, be a patient listener.

- When your child tells a story, use plenty of praise and support.

- Your child may "talk your ear off" and ask endless questions starting with "Why." Encourage this curiosity and interest.

- Together, look at a book that your child already knows. This time, let your child tell the story in his own way while you listen.

DID YOU KNOW?
Talking about their day helps children build storytelling skills. These skills help children understand what they read.

Shining the spotlight

Retell a favorite story using your child's name for the main character. If you have a recent photo of your child, you can actually put them into the book using the photo.

The color of the week

Once a week choose a color to highlight. Dress your child in that color; you should as well. Look for items around the house that are that color. What foods are that color? Construct a story using this information (for example: Michael got up and dressed in red pants and a red top. He went downstairs and ate strawberry jam on toast and drank cranberry juice for breakfast). Write down the story and help your child to illustrate it. You can draw the pictures or use digital images.

Try this at home!

IT'S STORYTIME!
Let's tell a story about your teddy bear's day (or other favorite stuffed animal).

- How do we get dressed? What goes on first? What goes on next?

- How do we get ready for bedtime?

- What is your favorite story? What is it about?

- Let's make up a story: Today we went to the library and…

Seeing Words

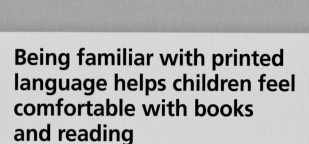

Being familiar with printed language helps children feel comfortable with books and reading

- Print awareness includes noticing that print is all around and has meaning.

- Before learning how to read a book, a child must learn what a book is, how words work, and how letters represent words.

- This chapter offers some ideas and activities to help your child become comfortable with printed language, books, and reading.

Developmental milestones

When books are available in the home, a child goes quickly from chewing a board book to enjoying both words and pictures.

Babies:

- Look at books and point to pictures

- Give books to adults to read to them

Toddlers:

- Scribble on paper with a purpose and tell you what they wrote or drew

- Begin to pay attention to specific print, such as the first letters of their names

- Turn books right side up; can turn pages with your help

Preschoolers:

- Identify familiar signs and labels

- Have an understanding of the function of print

- Know that print has a message

THE WHEELS ON THE BUS

Have your child copy your actions.

The wheels on the bus go round and round,
(Trace circles with index fingers)

Round and round, round and round.

The wheels on the bus go round and round,

All through the town.

Repeat the song substituting:

The doors on the bus go open and shut...
(Bring hands apart then together)

The people on the bus go up and down...
(Bounce up and down)

The driver on the bus says, "Move on back!..."
(Point toward back)

The babies on the bus go, "Wah, wah, wah..."
(Open mouth and wipe eyes with fists, as if crying)

The parents on the bus say, "Shh, shh, shh..."
(Put finger to lips for "Shh" sounds)

The wipers on the bus go swish, swish, swish...
(Palms face out, move them side to side)

The horn on the bus goes honk, honk, honk...
(Pretend to honk horn) (Repeat first verse)

You can adapt this song to your own car trips. For example: "The mommy in the car says, 'Buckle up! Buckle up! Buckle up!'" Invite your children to add their own silly verses to this song.

Pointing to words

Pointing to words as you read them helps your child become familiar with printed language.

- As you run your finger underneath the words, you show that the printed word and the story are connected.

- Books with large print or with few words on a page are especially good for pointing.

- Point to a word that interests your child and words that are repeated as you read them.

- Run your child's finger underneath the words as you read or, using a book that your child knows well, ask him to point to the words as you read them.

- These activities help your child see that, in English, we read from the top of the page to the bottom, from left to right, and that written words have a space between them. Your child is also learning that it's the print on the page being read, and not the pictures.

DID YOU KNOW?
Most books, rhymes, songs, and activities develop more than one skill.

Where should I start?

Before reading a story, introduce the cover and title, and talk about the author and illustrator.

Say things like, "Let's start at the beginning" and "Let's read the words."

First words

Up, down, in, out, fast, and slow are some of the first words in print that your child may start to recognize.

ROLY POLY, ROLY POLY

(Roll hands around each other.)

Roly poly, roly poly,

Up, up, up. Up, up, up.

Roly, roly, poly. Roly, roly, poly,

Down, down, down. Down, down, down.

Roly poly, roly poly,

Out, out, out. Out, out, out.

Roly, roly, poly. Roly, roly, poly,

In, in, in. In, in, in.

Roly poly, roly, poly,

Fast, fast, fast. Fast, fast, fast.

Roly, roly, poly. Roly, roly, poly,

Slow, slow, slow. Slow, slow, slow.

ONLINE VIDEO
Visit **torontopubliclibrary.ca/ readyforreading** to view video performances of fun rhymes like this one.

Read books

Read books with your child often.

- Any book with words helps develop print awareness because your child learns to recognize print, how books work, and how we use them.

- Let your child hold the book and turn the pages of the book as she "reads" to you or as you read together. Board books are good for babies to practice turning pages.

- Show your child that print is useful and that reading is important to you by talking to him about what you are reading: the newspaper, a book, a menu, a letter, or an email.

The Nonsense Show
Eric Carle, 2015
A colorful and hilarious book that begs to be read aloud about a fun, upside-down world.

It's Not Easy Being Number Three
Drew Dernavich, 2016
Number 3 is tired of his job and sets out to find more rewarding work, perhaps as a sculpture. A wonderful book about shapes and the importance of numbers.

Bouncing rhymes

These are good rhymes for a bounce or a gallop. Watch your child's face for clues to what she likes.

TO MARKET, TO MARKET

To market, to market, to buy a fat pig;
Home again, home again, jiggety jig.
To market, to market, to buy a fat hog;
Home again, home again, jiggety jog.
To market, to market, to buy a white cake;
Home again, home again, never was baked.
To market, to market, to buy a plum bun;
Home again, home again, market is done.
(Give your child a hug.)

BUMPIN' UP AND DOWN

Bumpin' up and down in my little red wagon.
Bumpin' up and down in my little red wagon.
Bumpin' up and down in my little red wagon.
Won't you be my darlin'!
One wheel's off and the axle's broken...
Freddie's gonna fix it with his hammer...
Laura's gonna fix it with her pliers...
Bumpin' up and down in my little red wagon.

✔ TIP

Be sure to give a baby's head extra support during bounces until he is strong enough to hold his head steady himself.

Print is all around

Even as a baby, your child will start to learn that printed words have meaning. Use every opportunity to read aloud.

- While walking or riding in a car, point to and talk about street signs, traffic signs and billboards. Praise your child when she recognizes words like "Stop" on stop signs or "Open" in shop windows.

- Point out labels while shopping. Point to and read print on toys, T-shirts, posters, and mugs.

- Other everyday print to read aloud might include lists, notes, letters, emails, menus, recipes, cereal boxes, directions, schedules, calendars, and birthday cards.

- Create a book with the signs, labels, and images your child is familiar with (favorite cereal, stop signs, etc). Your child will feel like a star when they can read the book by themselves.

Freight Train
Donald Crews, 1978
Enjoy this classic book filled with strong illustrations and simple words. A book to introduce children to the wonders of a train as it rolls by.

You Were the First
Patricia MacLachlan, 2013
Illus. Stephanie Graegin
A heartwarming story about baby's early milestones and moments parents hold dear to their heart.

The Seals on the Bus
Lenny Hort, 2000
Illus. G. Brian Karas
Following the pattern of "The Wheels on the Bus", join a series of wild animals as they travel on a city bus.

Scribble, write, and draw

Encourage scribbling, writing, and drawing in daily activities.

- Give your child opportunities to practice "writing" her name, a list, or notes. Encourage her to draw as well.

- Your child can draw a picture of what is happening in the book, or "write" words of a story.

- Share your own writing. For example, a shopping list is one way to show your child that printed words represent real things.

- Show your child how you write your shopping list (and let him "write" one too). At the store, read the list with your child and find the items together.

- Keep crayons and paper readily available where your child can write.

- With your child, write captions for pictures your child has drawn. This will help them make the connection between print and picture.

Signs, posters, and traffic lights

Show your child the street names. Does your child know where he lives?

TRAFFIC LIGHTS

Green means go,

Yellow means slow,

And red means STOP!

Lyrics reprinted by permission of Wendy Fine Music.

DO YOU KNOW THE MUFFIN MAN

Do you know the muffin man,

The muffin man, the muffin man?

Do you know the muffin man,

Who lives in Drury Lane?

Yes, I know the muffin man,

The muffin man, the muffin man.

Yes, I know the muffin man,

Who lives in Drury Lane.

HOW MUCH IS THAT DOGGIE IN THE WINDOW?

How much is that doggie in the window?

The one with the waggly tail.

How much is that doggie in the window?

I do hope that doggie's for sale.

–Bob Merrill

Language-rich environments

Print and books should be familiar and everyday items in your child's environment.

- Allow your child to explore books by keeping a variety of books within reach.

- Keep some books in your child's toy box.

- Start a little library for your child, keeping books on lower shelves.

- Get into the habit of carrying a small picture book with you all the time.

- Make a cosy nook just for reading together or alone.

- Show your child how you make lists or write notes.

- Make paper, pencils, markers, crayons, chalk, and finger paints available for scribbling, writing, and drawing.

- Visit the public library often and regularly for a fun outing. Get your child her own library card.

♣ *Drumheller Dinosaur Dance*
Robert Heidbreder, 2006
Illus. Bill Slavin and Esperança Melo
By day, the dinosaur bones in Drumheller rest, but by night they are ready to tango and dance until dawn. An exuberant read-aloud!

Please, Open This Book!
Adam Lehrhaupt, 2015
Illus. Matthew Forsythe
A monkey crew trapped between the pages of a book needs help. Opening the book is the only way to save them. A playful book that children will enjoy.

Play alien encounter

Pretend that you're from outer space and have never read a book before. Turn the book upside down, read it right to left, or mix the words up and allow your child to correct you. When the book is right-side up, explain that this will allow you to read it and start at the beginning. Use the words "front" and "back" of the book.

Play reporter

Let your child dictate to you as you write down his story, letter, or list. Read it back together and then switch roles.

Background and general knowledge

Background knowledge helps children understand what they are reading.

- Books, songs, and rhymes introduce new ideas that build your child's understanding of the world.

- Books often expose children to experiences outside their familiar environments and have pictures of things they may not see often.

- Gain knowledge together by reading books on many different topics.

- Non-fiction or information books use different words than those used in stories.

- Exposing your child to new information, and science and math concepts improves her reading comprehension.

- Play offers opportunities to practice new vocabulary and builds knowledge.

Where is it?

Babies can look and point to pictures in books. While reading a book together, stop and point to a word, and ask your baby where it is; such as, "Where is the red ball on this page?"

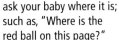

FIVE LITTLE DUCKS

This is a great song to sing during bath time with your child. If you have rubber duck toys, use these as props while you sing. This rhyme can help to teach children about counting and numbers.

Five little ducks went out one day,
(Hold up five fingers)

Over the hills and far away.
(Wave bye-bye)

Mother duck said, "Quack, quack, quack, quack,"

But only four little ducks came back.
(Hold up four fingers)

Repeat rhyme for:

Four little ducks went out one day...

Three little ducks went out one day...

Two little ducks went out one day...

One little duck went out one day...

Over the hills and far away.
(Wave bye-bye)

Mother duck said, "Quack, quack, quack, quack,"

But none of the five little ducks came back.
(Open hands in an "empty" gesture)

Sad mother duck went out one day,
(Sing it sadly and slowly)

Over the hills and far away.

Mother duck said, "QUACK! QUACK! QUACK! QUACK!"

And all of the five little ducks came back.
(Wave hand with all five fingers!)

Scavenger hunt

Create cards with words and pictures of things around the house. Have your child go on a scavenger hunt to find these items. Read the cards and pictures, showing your child the connection between the words, pictures and actual items.

DID YOU KNOW?
Children who recognize that reading is valuable will be motivated to learn how to read.

Who's Next Door?
Mayuko Kirish, 2014
Illus. Jun Takabatake

Chicken is excited that someone has moved in next door. But the new neighbor is never around. What could be keeping them apart?

I Feel Five!
Bethanie Deeney Murguia, 2014
Fritz can't wait to turn five! But when he realizes that everything still looks the same, he wonders if he ever will feel five.

❀ Fox and Squirrel Make a Friend
Ruth Ohi, 2014
A wonderfully illustrated picture book about new friendship, feelings, loyalty, and acceptance.

Sam & Dave Dig a Hole
Mac Barnett, 2014
Illus. Jon Klassen

Sam and Dave want to find something amazing during their dig but keep missing impressive jewels.

Rebus Books

In rebus books, stories, and rhymes, pictures or symbols are used instead of some words. This allows children to "read" using visual cues, and connects them to the other print words in the sentence. Rebus stories are a great way to make reading fun and exciting for children.

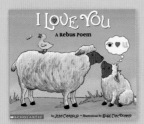

I Love You: A Rebus Poem
Jean Marzollo, 2000
Illus. Suse MacDonald

Simple text and pictures convey relationships between objects, animals, and people.

THE EENSY WEENSY SPIDER

Popular traditional nursery rhymes like this one appear in many videos and books that children may recognize.

The eensy weensy spider went up the waterspout.

Down came the rain and washed the spider out.

Out came the sun and dried up all the rain.

And the eensy weensy spider went up the spout again.

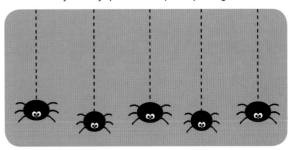

The Eensy Weensy Spider Freaks Out! (Big-Time!)
Troy Cummings, 2010
A humorous picture book about the eensy weensy spider that does not want to climb up the waterspout again.

Try this at home!

WHERE ARE THE WORDS HIDING IN YOUR HOUSE?

- Let's walk around the house and play a game of spot it. See who can spot it first!

- Look in your cupboards and find the words on labels that begin with the first letter of your child's name.

- Look through your bookshelf, and read the title of every book that has a blue spine. Make a list of your favorites.

Knowing Letters

Knowing the names and sounds of letters helps children to sound out words

- Learning about different shapes is a child's first step to learning the letters of the alphabet.

- To read, children must understand that written words are made of individual letters.

- Knowing the different sounds of letters helps children figure out how to say written words.

- This chapter offers some ideas and activities to help your child learn the names and sounds of letters.

Developmental milestones

A child needs to know the alphabet in order to read. Each child will learn at her own pace, but by age six almost all children will know all the letters and their sounds.

Babies:
- Explore shapes by touching and mouthing
- Learn to recognize and respond to their own names

Toddlers:
- Can match simple shapes with each other
- Start to use imaginary objects in play

Preschoolers:
- Start to match letters with sounds
- Recognize some letters, like the ones in their names

The alphabet song

A perfect song for teaching letter knowledge—anytime, anywhere!

THE ALPHABET SONG, OR THE ABC SONG
Sing to the tune of "Twinkle, Twinkle Little Star."

A, B, C, D, E, F, G,
H, I, J, K, L, M, N, O, P,
Q, R, S, T, U, V,
W, X, Y, and Z.
Now I know my A, B, Cs,
Next time won't you sing with me?

Display an alphabet in your home, and while you sing "The Alphabet Song," point to each letter or let your child do the pointing. This helps your child connect the name of the letter heard with the look of the letter.

Even if your child can sing "The Alphabet Song," she may still not have learned all the letters. It takes time to learn the look and sound of each letter.

Many different alphabet songs are available on CD to borrow from your local library.

 ONLINE VIDEO
Visit **torontopubliclibrary.ca/readyforreading** to view video performances of fun rhymes like this one.

 DID YOU KNOW?
Young children can hear the sound of a letter most easily when it is at the beginning of a word.

Your child's name

Talk about the letters that are most interesting to your child—the letters in his name.

- Help your child learn and recognize the first letter of her name. Together, look for that letter in a book. Eventually, your child will recognize and find all the letters of her name.

- Say the names of the letters as you print your child's name.

- Help your child write and read his own name.

- Print your child's name on labels for her toys or other personal items.

Useful play

Rhymes and songs can be useful playthings that help guide your child's actions. This funny little rhyme can ease children from a standing to a sitting position while building letter knowledge.

"A" IS FOR ALLIGATOR

"A" is for alligator, chomp, chomp, chomp.

"B" is for bouncing, up and down.

"C" is for circles, round and round.

"D" is for when we all sit down.

Round Is a Mooncake
Roseanne Thong, 2000
Illus. Grace Lin
Picking out the shapes of objects in this book is an excellent beginning step to letter knowledge.

Alphabet Everywhere
Elliott Kaufman, 2012
This book is a photographic alphabet hunt with the letters formed by buildings, shadows, and natural elements.

Circus 123
Guido Van Genechten, 2012
Welcome to the ladybug circus, featuring ladybugs on the trapeze and on bikes doing amazing circus tricks.

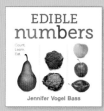

Edible Numbers
Jennifer Vogel Bass, 2014
Beautiful photographs illustrate items in the produce section of the grocery store. A delightful exploration of food and numbers.

Play with letters

Play games with alphabet blocks, felt, or foam letters, or letters cut from newspapers or magazines. Try making simple words or your child's name.

- Letters can also be made from string or cooked, cooled spaghetti. Your child may enjoy playing, writing, and drawing in sand, sugar, or flour.

- First trace a letter on paper (or sandpaper, for a tactile experience) with your finger and then use your child's finger to trace the shape of the letter. Can your child trace the letter without your help?

- Choose a "Letter of the Day" and point out everything you see, all day long, that starts with that letter.

- Find and name letters in books, on signs and labels, on toys, food boxes, and other objects all around.

- Help your child roll modeling clay or playdough into thin "logs." Ask your child to use the logs to form the letters he is learning.

- Play with magnetic letters on the refrigerator or on metal baking trays. Arrange the letters in alphabetical order. Remove a letter and ask your child which one is missing. Can she put the letter back into the correct space? Or, arrange the letters incorrectly and ask your child to put them into the correct order.

Interesting words

Help your child write and read words that interest him. Using magnetic letters, crayons, or pencil and paper, help him to write the names of family members, or words like "truck" or "book."

LETTER TILES

Use magnetic letters to create words with a pattern, such as "at." Change the first sound of the word by replacing the first letter with another. For example, change "cat" to "bat" by replacing the "c" with the "b."

RAINBOW NAME

Print your child's name on a piece of white paper. Ask your child to trace over the letters with different colors, until there is a rainbow around each letter of his name.

ME COLLAGE

Help your child look for the letters of her name in words on magazine pages. Cut out the letters and paste them down in order on paper. Now ask your child to look for words and pictures that tell about herself. Help to cut them out and paste them around her name.

Shape games

Learning about different shapes, and recognizing them, helps your child learn how letters are formed and prepares him to learn the alphabet.

- Help your child find shapes. What is round like a circle? A ball, a plate, a wheel? Can you find something shaped like a triangle? A slice of pizza? A piece of cheese?

- Introduce your baby to shapes by running her hand along the length of a spoon or along the curves of a ball and talk about the shapes you are feeling.

- Cut snacks into shapes. You could cut carrots or bananas into little circles or cut cheese into squares or triangles. Ask your child to identify the shapes.

- Show your child items in different colors and shapes. As you pick up each thing, describe it. For example, "This is a ball. It's round and in the shape of a circle. Do you see the big red ball?"

Rhymes with shapes

There are a number of rhymes, tickles, and bounces that include shapes.

THE MOON IS ROUND

The moon is round, as round can be,
(Trace your finger around child's face)

Two eyes, a nose, and a mouth—like me!
(Point to body parts and end with a smile or a kiss)

. . . .

ROUND AND ROUND THE GARDEN

Round and round the garden,

Goes the teddy bear.   *(Circle fingers around baby's tummy)*

One step. Two steps.   *(Walk fingers up chest)*

Tickle you under there!   *(Tickle baby under chin)*

. . . .

A GREAT BIG BALL

A great big ball,
(Make a circle by joining hands over head)

A middle-sized ball,
(Make a circle by touching fingers and thumbs of both hands together)

A little ball I see.
(Make a circle with thumb and index finger)

Let's see if we can count them:

One, two, three.
(Repeat motions above)

. . . .

CRISS-CROSS APPLESAUCE

Criss-cross,   *(Draw X on baby's back)*

Applesauce,   *(Tap shoulders 3 times)*

Spiders climbing up your back. *(Tickle baby's back)*

Cool breeze,   *(Blow on baby's neck)*

Tight squeeze,   *(Give baby a hug)*

Now you've got the shiveries!   *(Tickle all over)*

UPPER/lower case

The same letter can look different.

- Show and teach your child that there is a big "R" and a little "r"; a big "G" and a little "g".

- With any book, not just an alphabet book, you can point out specific letters and talk about them.

- Can your child find the same letter in upper case and lower case?

- Choose two letters: How do they look alike? How do they look different? What shapes do they have in them?

Mystery trip

Ask your child to pretend she is packing a suitcase or backpack for a special trip, but only things that start with the same "special letter" can go in. For instance, ask your child to pack items that begin with "f." Your child could pack flyers, a toy frog, and a frisbee. See how many items your child can find.

Play with puzzles

- Simple puzzles help preschoolers see differences between shapes.

- Help your child play with puzzles and encourage her to try a different space where the puzzle piece might fit.

- You can make your own puzzles by taking a picture, backing it with a piece of construction paper, and cutting it into different shaped pieces.

- Write your child's name on a strip of paper, leaving extra space between the letters. Cut apart the letters and mix them up. Ask your child to rearrange them in the order of her name. Play this game with other names or words of interest.

DID YOU KNOW?
Your child will develop Ready for Reading skills no matter what language you speak at home.

Mmmmm...

Sounds

Letter knowledge includes knowing that letters relate to sounds and that specific sounds go with specific letters.

- When you talk about letters, say the name of the letter as well as the sound it makes.

- Repeat letter sounds. "M" goes MMMMM. "B" goes BBBB.

- Knowing the sounds of the letters helps children figure out how to say written words.

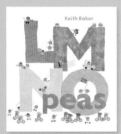

LMNO Peas
Keith Baker, 2010
A delightful alphabet book featuring small pea creatures that is sure to delight and entertain with rhymes and lovely illustrations.

One
Kathryn Otoshi, 2008
As budding young readers learn about numbers, counting and colors, they also learn about accepting each other's differences.

Same or different

Talk with your child about what is the same and what is different in things around you, or in the picture books you share.

MATCH-UPS

- Letting your child help you pair up socks from the laundry can help him to see the differences in shapes and patterns.

- Print upper case letters and clip each one to a clothespin. Ask your child to hang the letters and clothespins on a string, in alphabetical order.

- As a variation, search for fun letter-matching items to hang from each clothespin. For example, pin up a sock for "s," or a zipper for "z."

- Another variation: write each letter in lower case and ask your child to match them to the upper-case letters on the clothesline.

. . . .

LETTER TICKLERS

Tape a feather onto the end of a straw. After reading a page of a story, ask your child to "tickle" a letter. For example, ask your child to tickle all of the "r's" on a page from *Red is Best* by Kathy Stinson.

Books

Many books have print that is large and easy to read.

- Read books that feature shapes.

- Look at books where you have to find things (like *I Spy* books).

- Read alphabet books that link the letter to an object, such as: "A is for apple."

- Alphabet books do not need to be read from A to Z. You can let your child choose what letters and pictures to talk about. Listen, and then talk about the letter and its sound.

Using this rhyme, play with your child by passing their favorite toy or different objects back and forth between each number. You can choose to pass objects with different shapes, colors, and sizes and explore them with your child.

ONE POTATO

One potato, two potato,

Three potato, four,

Five potato, six potato,

Seven potato, more!

 DID YOU KNOW?
Helping your child learn the letters of the alphabet is one sure way to help him succeed at school.

Alphabet School
Stephen T. Johnson, 2015
Readers are invited to explore the alphabet through the shapes of everyday objects found at school, such as a ladder in the library for the letter "A."

Abigail
Catherine Rayner, 2013
Abigail loves to count. It is her very favorite thing, but when she tries counting Zebra's stripes and Cheetah's spots, they just won't sit still!

Sign Language ABC
Lora Heller, 2014
Introduce your child to signing the alphabet in this well-designed book with clear illustrations on how to use your fingers to spell words.

Alphabet up and down

Write down the ABCs mixed with both upper and lower case on a strip of paper. Sing the alphabet song with your child and stand up for upper case letters and sit down for lower case letters.

Letter hunt

With your child, go on a hunt for things in your house that start with a letter. You can choose to play with items in specific rooms. For example, if you start with the letter "a" and are playing in the kitchen, you can find an apple, an apron, and an avocado. Work your way through the alphabet until you get to "z."

B-I-N-G-O

This is a popular song that helps children learn to listen for different letters in the song.

There was a farmer, had a dog,
and Bingo was his name-o.
B-I-N-G-O
B-I-N-G-O
B-I-N-G-O
And Bingo was his name-o.

There was a farmer had a dog,
and Bingo was his name-o.
(clap)-I-N-G-O
(clap)-I-N-G-O
(clap)-I-N-G-O
And Bingo was his name-o.

Repeat rhyme for:
(clap)-(clap)-N-G-O...
(clap)-(clap)-(clap)-G-O...
(clap)-(clap)-(clap)-(clap)-O...
(clap)-(clap)-(clap)-(clap)-(clap)...
And Bingo was his name-o.

Feed the letter monster

Fill a paper bag or a resealable plastic bag with some magnetic letters and cut a hole to make a mouth in the middle. Add googly eyes, pompoms, and some other decorations to make it look like a monster. Play feed the monster by laying out a few magnetic letters in front of the monster and asking your child to feed the monster a specific letter. For babies, choose any of the letters and gently toss them in the monster's mouth, saying each letter out loud as the monster "eats" them.

Try this at home!

SEARCH AND FIND YOUR CHILD'S NAME

The letters in your child's name are most interesting to them. Find the letters to their name through these activities.

- Sing the alphabet song together and clap for each alphabet letter that appears in your child's name.
- Open a book and look for the letters in your child's name.
- Write your child's name on tape and label their toys.
- Write your child's name on a piece of cardboard and cut each letter out like a puzzle. Can you put the name together?

First & Best

Our top 50 picks of the best children's books for building reading readiness in kids under five. Because the first books you share with your child should also be the best!

Along a Long Road
Frank Viva, 2011

Baby's Lullaby
Jill Barber, 2010
Illus. HildaRose

Better Together
Sheryl and Simon Shapiro, 2011
Illus. Dušan Petričić

The Bus Ride
Marianne Dubuc, 2015

Chicken, Pig, Cow Horse Around
Ruth Ohi, 2010

Cinnamon Baby
Nicola Winstanley, 2011
Illus. Janice Nadeau

Drive: A Look at Roadside Opposites
Kellen Hatanaka, 2015

Eats
Marthe Jocelyn, 2007
Illus. Tom Slaughter

Extra Yarn
Mac Barnett, 2012
Illus. Jon Klassen

Farley Follows His Nose
Lynn Johnston and Beth Cruikshank, 2009
Illus. Lynn Johnston

Goodnight, Sweet Pig
Linda Bailey, 2007
Illus. Josée Masse

Grumpy Bird
Jeremy Tankard, 2007

Hana Hashimoto, Sixth Violin
Chieri Uegaki, 2014
Illus. Qin Leng

I Am So Brave!
Stephen Krensky, 2014
Illus. Sara Gillingham

I Dare You Not to Yawn
Hélène Boudreau, 2013
Illus. Serge Bloch

I Don't Want to Be a Frog
Dev Petty, 2015
Illus. Mike Boldt

In a Cloud of Dust
Alma Fullerton, 2015
Illus. Brian Deines

It's a Tiger!
David LaRochelle, 2012
Illus. Jeremy Tankard

Kiss, Tickle, Cuddle, Hug
Susan Musgrave, 2012

**Kitten's Autumn
Kitten's Spring**
Eugenie Fernandes, 2010

Little Panda
Renata Liwska, 2008

The Man with the Violin
Kathy Stinson, 2013
Illus. Dušan Petričić

Melvis and Elvis
Dennis Lee, 2015
Illus. Jeremy Tankard

Music is for Everyone
Jill Barber, 2014
Illus. Sydney Smith

My Blue Is Happy
Jessica Young, 2013
Illus. Catia Chien

One Watermelon Seed
Celia Barker Lottridge, 2008
Illus. Karen Patkau

Ones and Twos
Marthe and Nell Jocelyn, 2011

Out Came the Sun: A Day in Nursery Rhymes
Heather Collins, 2007

Over There
Steve Pilcher, 2014

A Paddling of Ducks: Animals in Groups from A to Z
Marjorie Blain Parker, 2010
Illus. Joseph Kelly

Peach Girl
Raymond Nakamura, 2014
Illus. Rebecca Bender

Ready for Winter
Ready for Spring
Ready for Summer
Ready for Autumn
Marthe Jocelyn, 2008
(board book set of 4, by season)

Red Wagon
Renata Liwska, 2011

Sam and Dave Dig a Hole
Mac Barnett, 2014
Illus. Jon Klassen

Same Same
Marthe Jocelyn, 2009
Illus. Tom Slaughter

Sidewalk Flowers
JonArno Lawson, 2015
Illus. Sydney Smith

Sing a Song of Mother Goose
Barbara Reid, 2007

So Many Babies
Lorna Crozier, 2015
Illus. Laura Watson

Sport-O-Rama
Benoit Tardif, 2015

The Sweetest One of All
Jean Little, 2008
Illus. Marisol Sarrazin

Thing-Thing
Cary Fagan, 2008
Illus. Nicolas Debon

Time Is When
Beth Gleick, 2008
Illus. Marthe Jocelyn

To the Sea
Cale Atkinson, 2015

Welcome, Baby
Barbara Reid, 2013

Welcome Song for Baby: A Lullaby for Newborns
Richard Van Camp, 2013

What Am I?
Linda Granfield, 2007
Illus. Jennifer Herbert

What Are You Doing?
Elisa Amado, 2011
Illus. Manuel Monroy

Who's Next Door?
Mayuko Kishira, 2014
Illus. Jun Takabatake

Wiggle Giggle Tickle Train
Nora Hilb and Sharon Jennings, 2009

Without You
Geneviève Côté, 2011

Research

Commitment to literacy

Every parent wants their child to succeed. Compelling studies show that to succeed in school, a child needs to be literate. Children begin to learn literacy skills as soon as they are born, long before they enter school. With your help as their first and best teachers, your children can start acquiring important literacy skills from birth.

Toronto Public Library, a leader in early literacy services in the community, modeled the *Ready for Reading* program and services on the American Library Association's initiative *Every Child Ready to Read @ Your Library*. Both are library-based programs that enlist parents and caregivers as key players in promoting early childhood literacy, giving them the information and the tools they need to help their children acquire the necessary skills.

Every Child Ready to Read and Toronto Public Library's *Ready for Reading* are founded on research into areas as diverse as national literacy statistics, school readiness studies, stages of brain development, and early childhood development.

Literacy

Adult literacy is a persistent problem, even in developed countries like the United States. According to the International Assessment of Adult Literacy, 43 percent of Americans read only at grade eight level or below. Low literacy can limit academic and career prospects, as well as the ability to cope in a modern society.[1]

School readiness

Research shows that an astonishing number of children are ill-prepared for school. The groundwork for success is laid by parents at home. Simple things such as reading regularly with your child, talking, using new words, and making books available at home can help overcome potentially negative setbacks, such as low socio-economic status. The relationship between the skills children have when they enter school and their later academic performance is striking. Children who start school without the necessary skills typically stay behind.

---

[1] OECD, *International Adult Literacy and Skills Survey*.

Brain development in early childhood

Scientists have found that the architecture of the brain develops in stages beginning before birth, and each stage of development builds on the previous one. In the first years of life, connections between brain synapses are made at an astounding rate. This is the time when babies are learning not only to crawl and walk, but also to make their first attempts to speak, relate to the world around them, and problem-solve. The more you communicate with your child in a supportive, stimulating, and nurturing environment, the more you nurture their brain development. Repeated messages mean more and stronger neural connections will be formed. And the easiest way to do this is by talking, reading, singing, playing, and writing with your child. This is a great way to build a solid foundation for future learning.

Literacy in early childhood

The *Every Child Ready to Read* initiative, which Toronto Public Library's *Ready for Reading* program is based on, demonstrates how to create simple, literacy-rich environments and experiences that are enjoyable and playful. It also emphasizes the importance of parents and caregivers as a child's first and best teachers, and suggests that everyday simple activities, such as talking, reading, singing, playing, and writing, help build pre-reading skills in children.

As new information comes forward, Toronto Public Library continues to make adjustments to its *Ready for Reading* programs based on the research.

Ready for Reading programs are built on these principles:

- Parents and caregivers are a child's first and best teachers, and the home is where the child begins to learn.
- Communication begins at birth.
- The parent-child relationship is the basis of the child's success.
- Parents and caregivers will benefit from knowing about their children's stages of development in language and literacy.
- Children learn through play.
- Everyday simple activities—such as talking, reading, singing, playing, and writing—help build pre-reading skills.
- The library supports and complements what families can do at home.

Recommended Books, Music, and Websites

Most titles included in this list are available to borrow at your local library, or can be purchased through your local bookstore or online.

Baby books

(Birth—18 months)

Animal Colors BB
little bee books, 2015
Let's go on a journey into the wild and learn our colors from the boldest and brightest animals.

Baby Can...Bounce!
Lynne Chapman, 2012
It's time to get up and get moving! A fun way for babies to learn words through movement and play.

Baby Look BB
Carol McDougall and Shanda LaRamee-Jones, 2012
A fold-out close-up look at baby faces and actions featuring a diverse set of babies.

Baby's First 123 BB
little bee books, 2015
Illus. Max and Sid
Counting from one to 10 has never been so much fun.

Baby Signs for Mealtime BB
Linda Acredolo and Susan Goodwyn, 2002
Illus. Penny Gentieu
Babies need to express themselves too. Communicate about your baby's mealtime needs using baby signing.

Baby's World: A First Book Of Senses BB
Dave Aikins, 2013
Learn about the five senses in this interactive touch-and-feel book.

Count: 1, 2, 3 BB
Simms Taback, 2009
A tiny book, for tiny hands to learn their numbers on the go.

Hello Baby: On the Go BB
Roger Priddy, 2013
Illus. Holly Jackman
A simple high-contrast board book that introduces children to vehicles on the go.

Lucy Cousins Treasury of Nursery Rhymes: Big Book of Nursery Rhymes and CD BB
Lucy Cousins, 2015
A collection of favorite nursery rhymes with music: From "Baa, Baa, Black Sheep" to "Bye, Baby Bunting".

Opposites BB
Sandra Boynton, 1982
From high and low to fast and slow, what better way to learn opposites than from these charming rhyming animals?

Peek-a-Baby: A Lift-the-Flap Book BB
Karen Katz, 2007
Is that Baby hiding behind the flaps? One, two, three, peekaboo!

Peekaboo Baby BB
Margaret Miller, 2001
What do babies love more than playing peekaboo? Playing peekaboo with other babies!

Rain, Rain, Go Away! BB
Caroline Jayne Church, 2013
Oh no, it's raining! Let's all read and sing the rain away.

Welcome, Baby
Barbara Reid, 2013
A wonderfully illustrated book to help welcome and celebrate the joys of having a newborn.

BB = Board Book

Wiggle Your Toes BB
Karen Katz, 2006

Have fun pointing to your nose and wiggling your tiny toes with this interactive board book.

Toddler books

(19 months—35 months)

♣ Baby Caillou Looks Around: The Seasons (a Toddler's Search And Find Book) BB
Anne Paradis, 2014

Illus. Pierre Brignaud

It's game time! Bring this book to the garden, the beach, or the park and see how many seasonal objects you can find.

Bear and Hare: Mine!
Emily Gravett, 2016

Bear wants to share, but Hare doesn't care. Will they learn to share?

Flaptastic: Colors BB
DK Publishing, 2009

A brightly illustrated book with interactive flaps that help introduce toddlers to colors and everyday objects.

In My Heart: A Book of Feelings
Jo Witek, 2014

Illus. Christine Roussey

An exploration of the many feelings—happiness, sadness, bravery, anger, and shyness—that our hearts can hold.

Leo Can Swim
Anna McQuinn, 2016

Illus. Ruth Hearson

Splishy splashy waves and puddles. Join Leo for some swim time fun!

Let's Make Faces
Hanoch Piven, 2013

The world is filled with faces. If you look carefully, you'll find faces in your garden, your garage, and even in vegetables!

Maisy's First Colors BB
Lucy Cousins, 2013

Eat your way through your first colors with Maisy and friends.

Mother, Mother, I Want Another
Maria Polushkin Robbins, 1978

Illus. Jon Goodell

Mrs. Mouse kisses her baby goodnight, but he cries, "Mother, Mother, I want another." So she rushes off to invite other mothers to help put baby mouse to sleep.

Nose to Toes, You Are Yummy!
Tim Harrington, 2015

It's time to get up and wave your hands and tap your feet. You're just in time for a jungle treat!

Now I Eat My ABC's BB
Pam Abrams, 2004

Illus. Bruce Wolf

It's time to eat, eat, eat, asparagus and blueberries!

Old MacDonald Had a Truck
Steve Goetz, 2016

Illus. Eda Kaban

Old MacDonald had a farm, E-I-E-I-O. And on that farm he had a…TRUCK?!

Spot's Favorite Colors BB
Eric Hill, 1997

Join Spot as he discovers different objects and colors he sees every day—from yellow bananas to purple butterflies.

Ten Little Dinosaurs
Mike Brownlow, 2015

Illus. Simon Rickerty

Roarrrrr! What happens when 10 little dinosaurs go on a noisy, rhyming adventure?

The Very Hungry Caterpillar's Christmas 123 BB
Eric Carle, 2015

Count the Christmas festivities with the much-loved Hungry Caterpillar.

Where's the Elephant?
Barroux, 2016

Where's the elephant? Where's the parrot? Where's the snake? A game of hide-and-seek that teaches children about deforestation.

Preschooler books

15 Things Not to Do with a Baby
Margaret McAllister, 2015

Illus. Holly Sterling

Don't give the baby to a kangaroo or swap him for the school guinea pig, and other rules for big sisters with little brothers.

The Eensy Weensy Spider Freaks Out! (Big Time!)
Troy Cummings, 2010

Out came the sun and dried up all the rain, and the eensy weensy spider said, "There's no way I'm climbing back up that gutter!"

Families, Families, Families
Suzanne Lang, 2015
Illus. Max Lang
A wonderful celebration of families of all sizes and shapes.

Five Little Monkeys Reading in Bed
Eileen Christelow, 2011
Five little monkeys are…reading in bed? Mama says, "Lights out! Sweet dreams." It's time for bed!

The Girl Who Heard Colors
Marie Harris, 2013
Illus. Vanessa Brantley-Newton
Some people, like Jillian, can hear the colors of music, voices, and other sounds.

Goldilocks and the Three Dinosaurs
Mo Willems, 2012
A witty retelling of the classic folktale starring three dinosaurs and Goldilocks.

I Can Do It Myself
Valorie Fisher, 2014
Practice new skills and celebrate the many things your child can do.

Isaac and His Amazing Asperger Superpowers!
Melanie Walsh, 2016
A highly informative book narrated by Isaac, a young boy who explains his world living with Asperger syndrome.

I Spy Pets
Edward Gibbs, 2013
Use the clues and look through the holes to see what animals you can spy with your little eyes.

Little White Fish
Guido van Genechten, 2015
A simple color association book that takes us on Little White Fish's search for his missing mommy.

Maybe a Bear Ate It!
Robie H. Harris, 2008
Illus. Michael Emberley
A little boy loses his book and imagines all the terrible things that may have happened to it.

The Pigeon Needs a Bath!
Mo Willems, 2014
Pigeon really needs to take a bath! Except, he doesn't think so, since he already took a bath last month! Can we convince him otherwise?

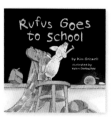

Rufus Goes to School
Kim T. Griswell, 2013
Illus. Valeri Gorbachev
Rufus wants to go to school and learn to read his favorite book. But he's a pig, and Principal Lipid says pigs aren't allowed at school.

The Very Itchy Bear
Nick Bland, 2011
Flea is biting Bear, high and low, but that's just how fleas say hello.

Who Has This Tail?
Laura Hulbert, 2012
Illus. Erik Brooks
A fun, informative book that begs you to guess the tails of different animals and see them in action.

CD suggestions

Barenaked Ladies
Snack Time!

Laurie Berkner
– *The Best of the Laurie Berkner Band*
– *Under a Shady Tree*

Charlotte Diamond
10 Carrot Diamond

Disney
Disney's Winnie the Pooh Lullabies

Ella Jenkins
Early, Early Childhood Songs

Bob McGrath
– *The Baby Record*
– *Songs & Games for Toddlers*

Michael & Jello
It Must be Jelly, 'Cause Jam Don't Shake

Hap Palmer
– *Early Childhood Classics*
– *Hap Palmer Sings Classic Nursery Rhymes*

Fred Penner
The Cat Came Back

Raffi
– *Everything Grows*
– *More Singable Songs for the Very Young*
– *Owl Singalong*
– *Singable Songs for the Very Young*

Kathy Reid-Naiman
– *More Tickles & Tunes*
– *A Smooth Road to London Town*
– *Zoom Zoom Cuddle and Croon*

Sharon, Lois & Bram
– *Great Big Hits*
– *One Elephant, Deux Éléphants*

Mike Whitla
Early Morning Knee-Slappin' Tunes

The Wiggles
Let's Eat!

Recommended websites

ABC Life Literacy
ABC Life Literacy Canada is a non-profit organization that inspires Canadians to increase their literacy skills. Visit this site for the latest news and information on family literacy, research, and programs.
http://abclifeliteracy.ca/family-literacy

¡Colorín Colorado! Getting Ready to Read
There are lots of things you can do at home to help your child get ready to read. A bilingual site in English and Spanish.
http://www.colorincolorado.org/help-your-child-learn-read

Every Child Ready to Read
The American Library Association website includes a review of the research upon which the Every Child Ready to Read program is based.
everychildreadytoread.org

Get Ready to Read
Use the Get Ready to Read screening tool with your child to see where she is with literacy skills. It is easy to use and most appropriate for children in the year before they enter kindergarten. Much of the content is also available in Spanish, Chinese, Korean, and Arabic.
http://www.getreadytoread.org

PBS Parents: Reading and Language
Learn how children become readers and writers and how you can help them develop by talking, reading, and writing together every day. Available in English and Spanish.
http://www.pbs.org/parents/readinglanguage/index.html

http://www.pbs.org/parents/readinglanguage/spanish/index.html

Reading Rockets: Launching Young Readers
Parents can find ways to help turn their young children into readers. This includes reading tips in 11 languages.
http://www.readingrockets.org/audience/parents

Ready at Five
Parent tips, parent-child activities, and school readiness resources, in English and in Spanish.
http://www.readyatfive. org/for-parents/spanish-resources.html

Storyblocks: Songs & Rhymes that Build Readers
Videos by the Colorado Libraries for Early Literacy, in English, French, Spanish, Vietnamese, and Arabic.
http://www.storyblocks.org/

Toronto Public Health
Find information about child development, nutrition, child safety, and resources for parents.
http://www1.toronto.ca/wps/portal/contentonly?vgnextoid=538f1291bfc30410VgnVCM10000071d60f89RCRD

Toronto Public Library
Good tips for parents on raising readers and choosing the right books for young children.
http://www.tpl.ca/readyforreading

TVO Parents: How to Read with Your Child
A series of videos on topics of interest to parents of preschoolers. This particular video is available in English, French, Spanish, Tamil, Urdu, Mandarin, Mohawk, and Cayuga.
https://www.youtube.com/watch?v=QULa903BOoo

U.S. Department of Education
Helping your child become a reader/ Cómo ayudar a su hijo a ser un buen lector. Available in English and Spanish.
http://www2.ed.gov/parents/academic/help/reader/index.html

http://www2.ed.gov/espanol/parents/academic/lector/index.html

Zero to Three
A wealth of information about the behaviour and development of children in their early years. Includes the publication "Getting Ready for School Begins at Birth" in English and Spanish.
https://www.zerotothree.org/early-learning/school-readiness

http://www.zerotothree.org

Storytime at the Library

Visit your local library branch today for storytime. Storytime at the library has bouncing and tickling rhymes, stories, songs, and activities for children with their parents and caregivers.

These programs help encourage a lifelong love of reading, build pre-reading skills in children, and show parents and caregivers how to help their children get ready for reading.

Summer Reading Clubs

Keep your kids reading all summer long.

This summer, visit your local library for great summer reading fun.

Here are some tips from public librarians to keep your kids reading all summer long:

- Read for fun, and let kids choose what to read.

- Read anywhere, anytime, and anything.

- Be a family of readers. Read together and read aloud.

- Start young. It's never too early (or too late!) to read with your children.

- Use your local library.

It's time to get a library card!

A library card gives a child a feeling of pride, ownership, and independence.

Plus, it helps further encourage a life-long love of books and reading.

Visit your local library to get one today.

Library Spaces

Public libraries are fun places for children and their caregivers to learn and play together.

Visit your local public library for many fun, free programs, warm spaces, and great books for you and your child to explore.

Image Credits

Book Covers

10: *Me and My Brother*; © Annick Press, 2007; *Caillou: My First ABC Alphabet Soup* © Chouette Publishing 2015; *Red is Best* © Annick Press, 2006;
12: *Where's the Elephant?* © 2016 by Barroux (reproduced by permission of the publisher, Candlewick Press, Somerville, MA); *Old MacDonald Had a Truck* © Chronicle Books, 2016; *Actual Size* © Houghton Mifflin Harcourt, 2004. **14:** *Ten Little Fingers and Ten Little Toes* © Houghton Mifflin Harcourt, 2008; *Tap the Magic Tree* © 2013 by Christie Matheson (used by permission of HarperCollins Publishers). **15:** *Little Penguin Gets the Hiccups* © 2015 by Tadgh Bentley (used by permission of HarperCollins Publishers); *This Book Just Ate My Dog!* © 2014 by Richard Byrne (reprinted by permission of Henry Holt & Company, LLC, all rights reserved); *Robot Smash!* © OwlKids Books, 2015. **16:** *If I Had a Triceratops* © 2015 by George O'Connor (reproduced by permission of the publisher, Candlewick Press, Somerville, MA); *The Monster at the End of This Book* © Golden Books, 1999; *The Baby Swap* © Little Simon, 2015. **17:** *A Birthday for Cow* © Houghton Mifflin Harcourt. **20:** *Out Came the Sun: A Day in Nursery Rhymes* © Kids Can Press, 2007; *Sing a Song of Mother Goose* © Scholastic Canada Ltd., 2008; *Brown Bear, Brown Bear, What Do You See?* 50th Anniversary Edition © 2016 by Bill Martin Jr./Illustrations © 2016 by Eric Carle (reprinted by permission of Henry Holt & Company, LLC, all rights reserved).
21: *Row, Row, Row Your Boat* © 2003 Child's Play (International) Ltd. (reproduced by kind permission of Child's Play [International] Ltd., www.childs-play.com, all rights reserved; *Shoe Shakes* © Annick Press, 2007. **23:** *Farmyard Beat* © Knopf Books for Young Readers, 2011; *Pete the Cat and His Four Groovy Buttons*, © James Dean (for the character of Pete the Cat)/© 2012 by James Dean and Eric Litwin (used by permission of HarperCollins Publishers); *Ladybugs Have Lots of Spots* © Annick Press, 2013. **24:** *Bee-bim Bop!* © Houghton Mifflin Harcourt, 2005; *Llama Llama Red Pajama* © Viking Books for Young Readers, 2005.
25: *We're Going on a Bear Hunt* © 1989 by Michael Rosen/Illustrations copyright © 1989 by Helen Oxenbury (reproduced by permission of the publisher, Candlewick Press, Somerville, MA, on behalf of Walker Books, London); *The Very Cranky Bear* © Scholastic Inc., 2009; *Sheep in a Jeep* © Houghton Mifflin Harcourt, 2003. **26:** *Sing a Song of Bedtime* © Scholastic Canada Ltd., 2015; *The Silver Moon: Lullabies and Cradle Songs*, Illustrations copyright © 2013 by Jui Ishida (used by permission of HarperCollins Publishers; *Read-Aloud Rhymes for the Very Young* © Dragonfly Books, 1986. **27:** *Your Baby's First Word Will Be Dada* © 2015 Jimmy Fallon (reprinted by permissions of Feiwel & Friends, all rights reserved). **30:** *Wiggle Your Toes* © Kids Can Press, 2011; *Eyes, Nose, Fingers,*
